I Have

by Cameron Grieft
illustrated by Eva Vagreti

Core Decodable 3

McGraw Hill Education

Bothell, WA • Chicago, IL • Columbus, OH • New York, NY

MHEonline.com

Send all inquiries to:
McGraw-Hill Education
8787 Orion Place
Columbus, OH 43240

ISBN: 978-0-02-145024-4
MHID: 0-02-145024-2

Printed in the United States of America.

7 8 9 LCR 25 24 23

I have .

cereal

I have  .

milk

I have  .

eggs

I have  .

orange juice

I have  .

toast

I have  .

jam